Fruitcake

Fruitcake

MEMORIES OF
TRUMAN CAPOTE
& SOOK

Marie Rudisill

Hill Street Press   Athens, Georgia

A HILL STREET PRESS/CLASSICS BOOK

Published in the United States of America by Hill Street Press LLC
191 East Broad Street, Suite 209   Athens, Georgia 30601-2848 USA
706-613-7200   info@hillstreetpress.com   www.hillstreetpress.com

The recipes in this book require careful preparation as well as the use of proper ingredients. Neither the author nor the publisher assumes any liability for the preparation and/or consumption of food prepared using the recipes included in this book.

Text design and illustrations by Anne Richmond Boston.

Printed in the United States of America.

The author wishes to thank Nathan Carter, John T. Edge, Damon Lee Fowler, Judy Long, and Hill Street Press.

PHOTO CREDITS:
Page 4:   Truman Capote with his beloved distant cousin, Sook Faulk, Monroeville, Alabama, circa 1928.
Page 22: Capote with his father, Archulus Persons, Monroeville, 1932.
Page 55: Page from 1866 farm journal kept by the Faulk family in Monroeville.
Page 79: Virginia Herd Faulk (Jenny), sole provider for Capote until he was seven years old, Monroeville, circa 1895.

All photos courtesy of the author.

Library of Congress Cataloging-in-Publication Data

Rudisill, Marie.
      Fruitcake : memories of Truman Capote and Sook / by Marie Rudisill.
         p.   cm.
      ISBN 1-892514-81-8 (alk. paper)
      1. Fruitcake. 2. Cookery, American—Southern style. 3. Capote, Truman,
   1924– I. Capote, Truman, 1924– II. Faulk, Sook, 1871–1946. II. Title.

   TX771.R83 2000
   641.8'653—dc21   00-058049

ISBN# 1-892514-81-8

10   9   8   7   6   5   4   3   2   1

First printing

For my son, Jim Rudisill

Contents

Introduction

These recipes were taken from a nineteenth century family farm journal owned by Sook Faulk, Truman Capote's distant cousin, who he immortalized in *A Christmas Memory*. The recipes are right to the point. Probably this is because times were hard in the Deep South after the Civil War. Some women were forced to work in the fields as well as run the household.

These recipes represent the history of our Southland. After the Civil War there were, of course, no mixes or short cuts for baking. It was a labor of love to make a cake. The actual baking was hard work. The oven of the big wood stove had to

be heated with a fire made from certain woods—white oak, hickory, or sassafras—depending on what was to be baked. Cooks had to know just what wood would produce a hot heat or a moderate heat. You will note that the baking instructions for temperature and time may vary with today's ovens. After the stove was heated, the fire had to be brushed out of the oven before cakes or breads could be baked. This was done with a large turkey feather. Only experienced bakers could tell by feel when the oven was ready to put the cakes in. Yet, in spite of all the difficulties, some wonderful recipes for sweets were handed down.

Marie Rudisill

from

A Christmas Memory

by

Truman Capote

Imagine a morning in late November. A coming of winter morning more than twenty years ago. Consider the kitchen of a spreading house in a country town. A great black stove is its main feature, but there is also a big

round table and a fireplace with two rocking chairs placed in front of it. Just today the fireplace commenced its seasonal roar.

A woman with shorn white hair is standing at the kitchen window. She is wearing tennis shoes and a shapeless gray sweater over a summery calico dress. She is small and sprightly, like a bantam hen; but, due to a long youthful illness, her shoulders are pitifully hunched. Her face is remarkable, not unlike Lincoln's—craggy like that, and tinted by sun and wind; but it is delicate too, finely boned, and her eyes are sherry-colored and timid. "Oh my," she exclaims, her breath smoking the windowpane, "It's fruitcake weather!"

The person to whom she is speaking is myself. I am seven; she is sixty something. We are cousins, very distant ones, and we have lived together—well, as long as I can remember. Other people inhabit the house, relatives; and though they have

power over us, and frequently make us cry, we are not, on the whole, too much aware of them. We are each other's best friend. She calls me Buddy, in memory of a boy who was formerly her best friend. The other Buddy died in the 1880s, when she was still a child. She is still a child.

"I knew it before I got out of bed," she says, turning away from the window with a purposeful excitement in her eyes. "The courthouse bell sounded so cold and clear. And there were no birds singing; they've gone to warmer country, yes indeed. Oh, Buddy, stop stuffing biscuit and fetch our buggy. Help me find my hat. We've thirty cakes to bake."

Sook Faulk's Fruitcakes

As Christmas time approached

Sook made elaborate fruitcakes, dark and blond, to

be given away to important people, and some not

so important. This undertaking required much

work and thought.

Sook would spread newspapers before the burning wood stove in her bedroom and measure out her pyramids of pecans, raisins, pineapple, cherries, brazil nuts, and maybe walnuts or almonds. You never knew just what fruitcake she was going to make. I would lie on her bed with Truman and watch her in the firelight, and I would quake deliciously inside, my nose twitching like a rabbit. Sook started making fruitcakes in 1921 when she was fifty years old and continued until 1945 when Truman was around twenty-one years old. She sent them to several presidents, Roosevelt being one of her favorites. Sook and Truman hauled the fruitcakes

that were to be given out to folks in Monroeville, Alabama, in a little wicker doll carriage. Some went to Rooktown, the black community, as well as to many needy families.

Two fruitcakes always went to Victoria, an Apache Indian that ran a fish camp on Little River. He supplied Sook with the whisky with which to ply the cakes. He was given two fruitcakes in return. He is the character, Mr. Haha Jones, in Truman's *A Christmas Memory*.

The Queen of Cakes

Fruitcakes have been belit-

tled long enough. As Christmas approaches, it is

time to stand up for that wonderful concoction of

walnuts, pecans, candied red and green cherries,

pineapples, dates, almonds and such. It has been a

hard pull for fruitcakes, however, they have come a long way. They are no longer just for Christmas. They are served at afternoon teas, at picnics on the grounds, or at home with a steaming cup of coffee and a good book.

Fruitcakes are true ambrosia—the queen of cakes. My happiest memories are associated with that old red tin fruitcake container which sat on a high shelf in the kitchen pantry. On Christmas Eve we could wait no longer. Silently, we pried off the tight lid and almost fell out over the fumes from the brandy. Without remorse, we plunged a fork into the dark flesh of the fruitcake, knowing full well we would answer for our act. Well, it was Christmas time, and everybody would be in a gay and forgiving mood. There was only one thing to do—enjoy!

Pointers for Fruitcake Baking

Fruitcake, to Southerners, is a birthright.

The most important ingredient in fruitcake baking is your choice of flour. Growing up in the Deep South, we were taught to use the very best of everything and that a Southern dinner always ends with dessert.

FRUITCAKE

It is only natural that White Lily All-Purpose Flour would be chosen for testing these fruitcake recipes. White Lily is a trademark of the White Lily Foods Company. White Lily began in 1883 and is proud to be 115 years old. It is not strange that a recipe from 1866 would unite with flour from 1883!

White Lily is known as "the light baking flour" because it is made up of 100% pure soft winter wheat. Fruitcakes by any standard, are heavy . . . so, a light flour would definitely be a plus!

- ❦ For the best flavor, make fruitcakes four to six weeks ahead of time.
- ❦ Plan to chop fruits and nuts one day, then mix the batter and bake the next day.
- ❦ Place shallow pan of hot water on the bottom of the oven while baking and you will have a moist cake.

- ❦ Always cool the fruitcake in pans, then turn out.
- ❦ Wrap the cakes in a brandy, wine, or juice-soaked cloth.
- ❦ Be sure to moisten again once a week.
- ❦ Store the cakes in airtight containers.
- ❦ Keep in cool place.
- ❦ Chill before slicing, for thin, perfect slices.
- ❦ Use a straight edged, thin bladed knife. Dip knife in hot water and cut with slow, sawing motion.
- ❦ To decorate the fruitcake brush the top with hot corn syrup and trim with candied cherries, nuts, gumdrops, etc. When set, brush with a second glaze. Allow the glaze to dry before wrapping.
- ❦ Repeat! Fruitcakes slice best when refrigerated before use.

1866 Fruitcake

Originally known as the "Lee Fruitcake."

This recipe was found in Bud Faulk's dresser drawer, folded up inside his copy of A Life of General Robert E. Lee by John Estes Cook. Bud was born in 1869 and was a collector of everything that had to do with the Civil War.

The story goes that a shed rattlesnake skin was found in the same dresser drawer. Household workers claimed that the snake lived in the drawer during Bud's lifetime and followed him to his grave when he died. To this day when you go to the graveyard you will always see a rattlesnake coiled on top of Bud's grave.

FRUITCAKE

1/2 cup candied lemon peel

1/2 cup sliced candied
    orange peel

1-1/2 cups finely cut citron

1-1/2 cups candied pineapple

1 cup candied cherries

1-1/4 cups dark seeded raisins

1-1/4 cup white raisins

1 cup chopped California walnuts

1 cup chopped pecans

1/4 cup sifted enriched flour

1 cup butter

2 cups brown sugar

4 eggs

2-1/2 cups enriched flour

1 teaspoon baking powder

1 teaspoon salt

1 teaspoon all spice

1 teaspoon cinnamon

1/2 teaspoon nutmeg

1/2 teaspoon cloves

3/4 cup grape juice

Combine the peels, fruits, nuts; sprinkle with 1/4 cup of flour and mix well.

Thoroughly cream butter and sugar. Add eggs and beat well. Sift together 2 cups of flour, the baking powder, salt, and spices; add alternately with grape juice. Pour the batter over the floured mixture of peels, fruits, and nuts.

Pour into a large tube pan until 3/4 full. Do not flatten batter. Bake in a very slow oven at 250° F for about 5 hours. Remove from pan and pack in air tight tin with a double layer of cheese-cloth soaked in bourbon.

Bake at least 3 months before Christmas. Do not let the cake dry out and keep lacing it with bourbon.

Birthday Fruitcake

3-1/4 cups flour

1 teaspoon baking powder

1 cup butter

1/3 cup light cream

4 eggs

1/4 teaspoon salt

1 cup super fine sugar

1/3 cup light corn syrup

1/4 cup light rum

2 teaspoon vanilla extract

1-1/2 cups candied fruits, diced

1 cup chopped walnuts

3/4 cups dark raisins

1/2 cup white raisins

3/4 cups currants

butter for greasing cake pans

Sift 3 cups of flour together with the baking powder in a large mixing bowl.

Add the butter and cream together until thoroughly blended. Beat the eggs with the salt and

sugar until light and thick. Add the egg mixtures to the flour mixture and mix until well blended. Add the syrup, cream, rum, and vanilla.

In a bowl mix the candied fruits, nuts, raisins, and currants with the remaining 1/4 cup of flour. Stir all of these ingredients into the batter.

Place the batter into 2 well buttered 9 x 5 x 3-inch loaf pans and bake in a preheated 350°F oven for 10 minutes.

Reduce the oven temperature to 325°F and continue baking for 1-1/2 hours, or until the cakes test done. To keep the cakes from burning on top place a piece of aluminum foil over each pan after 20 minutes of baking-time.

When that cakes have cooled, wrap them tightly in aluminum foil. They should be kept a few days before eating to improve flavor and texture.

The Origin of the Fruitcake

Romans and Spaniards baked nut and spice cakes and carried them northward across Europe. The Greeks called fruitcake the "food of the gods" as early as 300 B.C. It is believed that fruitcakes originated in ancient

Egypt. The Egyptians made dark cakes with sun dried fruit, nuts, dates, figs, and pomegranates. The cake mixture was made from hand ground flour, honey and spices. These cakes were buried with individuals for their use in the afterlife.

Fruitcakes were discovered in the Orient and on the Mediterranean by sailors from Great Britain. They brought back preserved and dried fruits, spices and nuts which they added to their traditional bread cakes. These were the first English fruitcakes.

Bride's Fruitcake

3/4 cup butter

2 cups sugar

1 teaspoon vanilla extract

2 cups cake flour

1/2 teaspoon salt

4 teaspoons salt

1 cup milk

6 stiff beaten egg whites

1/2 cup chopped blanched
       almond meats

1/4 cup chopped citron

1/4 cup chopped candied cherries

Thoroughly cream butter and sugar, add vanilla.
Add the flour, sifted with salt and baking powder,
alternately with milk. Fold in egg whites, then nut
meats and fruit.

Bake in 2 wax paper-lined 10-inch layer cake
pans at 350°F for 30 minutes or until they test
done.

Chocolate Fruitcake

1/2 cup shortening

1 cup sugar

3 eggs

3 one ounce squares unsweetened chocolate, melted

2 cups sifted all-purpose flour

2 teaspoons baking powder

1 teaspoon salt

1 teaspoon cinnamon

1/8 cup milk

3 cups mixed chopped candied
fruits and peels

1 cup raisins

1 cup broken California walnuts

Cream shortening and sugar. Add eggs, 1 at a
time, beating well; stir in chocolate.

Sift together dry ingredients; add to creamed
mixture alternately with milk. Stir in fruit and
nuts.

Pour into a greased, paper lined 10-inch tube pan. Bake at 275°F for 1-3/4 hours or until cake tests done.

Cool; remove from pan. Wrap in cheesecloth that has been soaked in sherry, bourbon or brandy. Surround with apples and enclose in a container that is airtight. Every few weeks repeat the dousing with the liquor of your choice.

Where the Christmas Wild Things Grow

$\mathcal{A}$ few days before Christmas when the weather was cold and full of angry showers and blistery winds we took off for the woods to look for our Christmas wild thing.

Sook; Bud, her brother; Truman; Spider, the

grandson of Sylvester, who worked for Bud on his farm; and myself would pack a lunch of fried chicken, cucumber sandwiches, coffee, and our first fruitcake of the season.

We would go to the woods back of Bud's farm, where there were big gullies and the aspen trees grew. Aspen trees grow together in little groups, straight, slender and white. They twinkle and murmur even when there is no wind. These little trees gave Truman the name for a story . . . he called it "Music of the Saw Grass." Truman eventually expanded the story into the novella, *The Grass Harp*.

We would all select our tree, except Bud who would remain on the ground to make the coffee and spread the lunch. I can see Sook now—tucking her skirt up under her long drawers and climbing her tree.

Our rules for climbing were: You must climb

high enough in your tree that it wobbles. Put your foot-weight lightly on the frail branches and let them lunge and grip the wind. It will beat you up, slapping your hair in your eyes, stinging your face with bark, trying to break your hold. You will know what it is like to be in a hurricane.

We would ride the trees until the wind had died down and the trees settled back to gently swaying and murmuring.

Bud would have the coffee made and the lunch laid out on the ground. The old red Christmas tin would be opened and we would eat our first fruitcake before Christmas!

Christmas Fruitcake

This recipe is said to have been copied from Martha Washington's own book. Written by the side: "The true fruitcake should contain but little batter in proportion to its fruit. It should be black, rich and moist and to achieve this result must be baked very slowly, five hours at the least, in order to give the fruit time to swell and its juices to permeate the entire mass. Such cake will keep for years if put in a cool place in a stone jar."

It is interesting to read about some strange methods of measuring in the early 1800s recipes:

Salt: As much salt as will lie on a nickel.

Butter: As much butter as the size of a walnut; or the size of an egg or a lump.

Molasses: Measure by globs.

1/2 pound butter

1-1/2 pounds sugar

6 eggs separated

1 pint sour cream

1 teaspoon soda

1-3/4 pounds flour

1 pound seeded raisins

1 pound currants

1/2 pound citron

juice of 1 lemon

rind of 2 lemons

1 nutmeg, grated

mace

Cream together butter and sugar. Add gradually 6 beaten yolks until creamy; then add the sour cream in which a teaspoon of soda has been dissolved, alternating with 1-1/2 pounds of flour. Next, add the whites of the 6 eggs, beaten stiff.

Lastly, add seeded raisins, currants, citron dredged with a 1/4 pound of flour. Add the lemon juice and the rind, nutmeg and a sprinkling of mace.

Bake in a greased 10-inch tube pan for 5 hours at a slow, steady heat. Cover with buttered paper while baking.

Civil War Fruitcake

Due to the scarcity of ingredients during and after the war—this was a great favorite. Like most fruitcakes, the Civil War Fruitcake improves with age. Most cooks liked to "feed the cake" every week during the aging period with a teaspoon of brandy or bourbon.

1 cup unsalted butter	1/2 cup warm water
3 cups golden raisins	Pinch of salt
2 cups brown sugar, firmly packed	1/3 teaspoon pure vanilla
1 teaspoon allspice	4 cups flour (wheat if possible)
	2 eggs well beaten

Melt the butter, stir in the raisins, sugar, allspice, water, salt and vanilla, and bring to a boil. Turn down the heat and simmer for 10 minutes. Take off the heat and allow the mixture to cool. Add the flour and beaten eggs, mix well.

Pour the mixture into a 10-inch cake pan, greased and lined with wax paper and bake at 250°F for 2 hours, until golden brown.

If you dare!
Taken from an old cookbook of the early 1800s:

"A sure way of testing a cake in the oven is to draw it to the edge of the oven and put the ear close to it. When the cake is not sufficiently baked, a slight sputtering noise will be heard, but when thoroughly baked there will be no sound."

Claiborne Fruitcake

Claiborne, Alabama is located in Monroe County on the banks of the Alabama river. As you ride down the sloping road that leads to the river, you are impressed with the fact that it is two hundred feet above the river. It is sort of scary because all of a sudden you are on the banks of the river. Some find the surly, dark river romantic as you watch the innumerable clear springs that issue from the bluff and throw themselves headlong into the river below. Every few years the river rises and flows over the banks to sweeten the earth. The earth around the river is dark and rich, sweet smelling from the bowels of the river. Claiborne claims fame due to the visit of the French General Marquis de Lafayette on April 5th, 1825.

He was honored for his aid to the American colonists in their fight for freedom. The letter of invitation to visit Claiborne, written by James Dellet, a congressman from the Whig party, follows:

General Lafayette
Sir:

The citizens of the county of Monroe and town of Claiborne, having participated in common with the American people, in the unfeigned gladness of heart imparted by the certain information of your arrival in the United States, desire me to say to you that it will afford them gratification which they anticipate with the grateful feelings, if you can make it convenient to touch at Claiborne on your passage from Montgomery and Mobile and afford them the pleasure of your company for such time as you can spare

under the arrangements of your Western tour.

I am with very great respect,

Your Obt. James Dellet
Chairman of the Committee of Claiborne
21st of March 1825

General Lafayette and his entourage, with his son, George Washington Lafayette, traveled by boat on the Alabama river from Montgomery to Mobile and spent the afternoon and evening in Claiborne as a result of this invitation.

A reception was held at the Dellet home. No expense was spared. The menu consisted of six hams, eight roast turkeys, six roasted suckling pigs, twenty-four hens, twelve ducks, and six roast beef with all the other trimmings.

The Claiborne fruitcake is moist and light and will cut into even, fruit studded slices.

1-1/2 cups chopped candied cherries

1 cup chopped candied pineapple

1/2 cup chopped candied citron

1/2 cup chopped candied lemon peel

1/2 cup chopped candied orange peel

1 cup chopped walnuts

3 cups sifted flour

1 cup pure butter

1 cup sugar

4 eggs

1/4 cup light corn syrup

1/4 cup orange juice

1/4 cup best sherry

Combine fruits and nuts; coat well with 1 cup of flour.

Cream butter and sugar together, till light and fluffy. Add eggs, one at a time, beating well after adding each. Combine corn syrup, orange juice and sherry; add alternately with remaining flour to creamed mixture. Fold in fruits and nuts.

Pour batter into well greased 4-1/2 x 2-5/8 x 2-inch baking pans to make 8 small loaves. Bake 70 minutes at 275°F.

Coconut Fruitcake

2 cups chopped nuts-pecans, walnuts

1-1/2 cups snipped pitted dates

1 cup candied cherries

1 cup candied pineapple

1/2 cup candied orange peel

1/2 cup candied lemon peel

2 cups sifted all-purpose flour

1 teaspoon salt

1 teaspoon baking powder

1 teaspoon ground allspice

1/2 teaspoon ground nutmeg

1/2 teaspoon ground cloves

1 cup butter

1/2 cup sugar

1/2 cup honey

5 eggs

1/3 cup orange juice

1 cup raisins

1-1/3 cups flaked coconut

Shake nuts, dates and candied fruits in 1/4 cup of the flour; sift together the remaining flour, the salt, baking powder, and spices.

Cream together the butter and sugar, stir in the honey. Beat in eggs, 1 at a time, beating well after adding each. Add the dry ingredients to the creamed mixture alternately with the orange juice; stir in raisins and coconut.

Pour the batter over floured candied fruit mixture; mix well. Bake at 275°F for about 3 hours in a large loaf pan or 2 small loaf pans.

Farmer's Fruitcake

3 cups dried apples

1 cup water

2 cups molasses

1 cup butter

1 cup brown sugar

1 pound raisins

1/4 pound citron

2 eggs

1 lemon (both juice and rind)

2 teaspoons soda

1 pound and 1 small cup flour

Soak the apples overnight in 1 cup of water, chop fine, then boil until done in the molasses and the water in which they were soaked.

Combine boiled apples with remainder of ingredients. Bake 3 hours at 250°F. Flavor with cinnamon, nutmeg and a little clove.

Festive Table Decorations

When decorating your table, do not make the mistake of setting out a "token" decoration, for it is as depressing as serving a "token" meal. It is far better to do without a centerpiece.

❦ Whistler and Oscar Wilde created a mania

for blue China pots in which they placed
aquilegia and iris.

🍒 Proust, although he admired chrysanthe-
mums, placed orchids on his dinner table.

🍒 Imagination is the most important ingredient
in choosing your table decorations. Why not
try the architectural parterres of ruby red
radishes, small spring onions, and purple
turnips, along with pyramids of strawberries
with leaves?

Festive Fruitcake

1 cup pure butter

1 cup granulated sugar

1 cup firmly packed brown sugar

4 eggs

2 cups applesauce

4 cups all-purpose flour

1 teaspoon salt

1 teaspoon baking powder

2 teaspoons cinnamon

1 teaspoon mace

2 teaspoons nutmeg

2 tablespoons unsweetened cocoa powder

1 pound raisins

1 pound mixed candied fruit

1/2 pound candied cherries

1/2 cup chopped English walnuts

1/2 cup pecans

Juice and peel of 1/2 fresh orange

Juice of 1 lemon

Combine sugar, brown sugar and butter in a large bowl; cream until well blended. Add eggs, 1 at a time; add applesauce.

Sift 3 cups flour, salt, baking powder, cinnamon, mace, nutmeg, and cocoa together. Combine with applesauce mixture. Stir until well blended.

Coat raisins, candied fruit and nuts with remaining 1 cup flour; stir mixture into batter and mix thoroughly. Stir in orange juice, orange peel, and lemon juice.

Pour into a large greased tube pan and bake at 275° F for 3 to 4 hours. Place a shallow pan of water in the bottom of the oven while baking.

Remove cake from pan and wrap in several layers of cheesecloth. Soak well with wine and brandy and pack in airtight containers. Best when stored about 3 months before eating.

Golden Fruitcake

1 cup dried apricots
boiling water
2 cups chopped candied
    pineapple
2 cups gold raisins
1 cup dark raisins
1 cup halved candied cherries
1 cup chopped citron
1 cup chopped candied
    orange peel
1/2 cup chopped lemon peel

2 cups chopped pecans
1 cup shaved almonds
1-1/4 cups shortening
1-1/2 cups honey
2 teaspoons rum extract of
    vanilla
6 eggs
2-1/2 cups sifted, all-purpose
    flour
1-1/2 teaspoons salt
1 teaspoon cloves

FRUITCAKE

Cut apricots in thin slices; cover with boiling water. Let stand 20 minutes and drain. Combine with the next 9 ingredients (pineapple through almonds).

Cream shortening, honey, and rum extract of vanilla until light; beat in eggs. Sift together flour, salt, and cloves. Add to creamed mixture, mixing to smooth batter. Fold in fruit and nut mixture.

Turn into a greased 10-inch tube pan and (1) 7-1/2 x 3-3/4 x 2-1/3-inch loaf pan. Bake at 275°F for about 3 hours; place a shallow pan of hot water on the bottom of the oven.

Let the cakes cool and remove from pans. Wrap in fruit juice-soaked cloth and store in cool place in airtight containers. Keep for several weeks before eating. Decorate with holly leaves and pecan halves.

Honey Fruitcake

1-1/2 cups butter

2 cups light brown sugar

1/2 cup honey

6 eggs

5 cups mixed candied fruits

2 cups golden raisins

1-1/2 cups chopped pecans

4 cups flour

2 teaspoon baking powder

1 teaspoon salt

1 teaspoon cinnamon

1 teaspoon nutmeg

1/2 teaspoon baking soda

1/2 teaspoon cloves

1/3 cup sherry

In a large bowl work butter until it is soft and add gradually the light brown sugar. Work until smooth. Add honey and eggs, 1 at a time, beating well. Mix in candied fruits, raisins, and pecans.

Sift together flour, ginger, baking powder, salt, cinnamon, nutmeg, baking soda, and cloves. Stir the spiced flour into the fruit mix, alternately with sherry.

Pour the batter into a greased 10-inch tube pan, line with brown paper and grease again. Bake in a slow oven at 300°F for about 4 hours.

Put the cake on a wire rack until it is almost cool, remove from the pan and peel off paper. Wrap the cake in sherry soaked cheesecloth and store in an airtight container for about a month.

HOW DOES A BEE MAKE HONEY?

A girl bee makes honey in a special stomach. First, she goes to a flower for the makings. She sips the sweet flower juice called nectar up through her mouth, which is shaped like a tiny soda straw down into her honey stomach where it becomes the most healthful

kind of sweet. If she ate all the honey herself, she would get too fat to fly. So she wings back to the hive to feed the baby bees a delicious treat called bee bread made out of honey mixed with flower pollen.

Leftovers go into the honeycomb. The bee then seals the comb with wax which she also makes herself.

Note: This was written by the side of this recipe by someone in our family who thought it would be of interest.

Ladies Fruitcake

This fruitcake was served by ladies of quality during the 1800s with tea or a glass of sherry wine.

1 cup shredded, blanched toasted almonds

1 cup flaked coconut

1-1/2 cups golden raisins

1 cup candied pineapple, cut in fine pieces

1/2 cup candied citron, cut in fine pieces

1 cup halved red candied cherries

1 teaspoon grated lemon rind

1 cup butter

2 cups sugar

2 tablespoons fresh lemon juice

1/3 cup fresh orange juice

3-1/2 cups all-purpose flour

1/2 teaspoon salt

1 teaspoon soda

6 egg whites

Combine nuts, coconut, fruit, and lemon juice in mixing bowl and toss well.

Cream butter well, then cream in sugar gradually until light-colored. Add juices alternately with flour that has been sifted with salt and soda. Add fruit juices and turn over repeatedly until well-mixed. Beat egg white until stiff but not dry.

Immediately pour into 2 large loaf pans lined with buttered wax paper. The paper will prevent the sides and bottom of the cake from darkening. Bake at 275°F for approximately 1 hour. Let cool about 2-1/2 hours and when dry brush well with liquor. Keep about 1 month before serving.

Peacock Fruitcake

1-1/2 cups red candied cherries, chopped

1 cup light raisins

1 cup candied pineapple

1/2 cup green candied cherries

1/2 cup candied lemon peel

1/2 cup orange peel

1 cup walnuts, chopped

3 cups sifted all-purpose flour

1 cup pure butter

1 cup sugar

4 eggs

1/4 cup light corn syrup

1/4 cup orange juice

1/4 cup best sherry

Combine chopped fruits, peels, and nuts. Mix in 1 cup of the flour.

Cream butter and sugar till light; add eggs, 1 at a time, beating well after each addition.

Combine corn syrup, orange juice, and sherry; add alternately with remaining flour to creamed mixtures. Fold in fruit and nuts.

Pour into 2 well-greased 5-1/2 cup ring molds. Bake at 275° F for 1-1/4 hours.

THE FABULOUS FAN-DANCER—THE PEACOCK

We always kept peacocks, and it is true that once you have one you are hooked for life. The beauty of the peacock's fan-shaped tail train, with its spectacular sunburst of color, is so inspiring you feel something vital has gone from your life when the rainbow bird is not around. Sook created this fruitcake, naming it the "peacock fruitcake," because when it is sliced very thin, the many vibrant-colored fruits resemble the fabulous fan dancer—the peacock.

Kitchen of Truman's and My Childhood

In the time of Truman's and my

childhood, the kitchen was the most important

place in the Faulk household, which was run by

our distant cousin, Jenny. The big black cook stove

was like an altar with its lofty turreted range

trimmed with nickel and the name, "Old Buckeye," cast on the front of the big oven door.

On one of the many lidded eyes sat a blue splatter-ware coffee pot which usually contained an egg shell used for clarifying the coffee. There was always hot coffee. The coffee aroma mingled with the smoke, lighter wood, and whatever was cooking—a parade of fragrances steamed up from the cavernous ovens and big iron pots. The fire winked through the glass dampers like jewels of various colors.

We all gathered around to help with chores and watched Anna Stabler blacken the stove about once a week. Anna would bring out a tin of cake polish and a brush. The cooler the stove, the better the polish worked. We used crumpled newspapers to polish the surface and to make it shine like a mirror. When the fire was rebuilt the stove smelled of baking polish until the fire got bright.

Anna kept an old turkey feather to brush the top of the stove, and no matter how quickly we swiped across the hot lids, the feathers always got singed a little. Jenny would scream at Anna, "Keep that kid [Truman] away from that stinking stove. He might set the house on fire. Besides, you know how burned turkey feathers stink."

Anna Stabler was not afraid of any person, white or not. She was a privileged character for she had been with the family for many, many years. The kitchen belonged to her and she let Jenny know it pretty quick.

How we loved the old stove. There was always something on one of the eyes or up in the warming compartment on the very top—cornbread or biscuits.

—Jim Rudisill

Pecan Fruitcake

In the South there is an abundance of pecans. One of the joys of childhood was climbing a giant tree and shaking the pecans down to the people below.

2/3 cup butter

3/4 cup sugar

pinch of salt

3 eggs

2 cups sifted flour

1/2 teaspoon baking powder

1 cup dried apricots, softened in boiling water, drained and cut into small pieces

1 cup coarsely chopped pecans

1 cup golden raisins

1 slice chopped, candied pineapple

grated rind of 1 lemon

grated rind of 1 orange

In a bowl cream butter well and gradually add sugar and salt, beating the mixture until it is smooth. Add eggs, one at a time. Stir in flour, sifted with baking powder. Add apricots, pecans, raisins, pineapple, lemon rind and orange rind.

Pour the batter into a large loaf pan lined with wax paper brushed in oil. Bake the cake in a slow oven at 325°F for about 3 hours.

Remove the cake from the pan and peel off the wax paper. Let the cake cool completely and store it in an airtight container to mellow for several months. From time to time, soak cheesecloth in brandy or wine and wrap around the cake.

THE PECAN

The pecan, with its graceful, elongated shape and its smooth brown texture, has an amiable appearance. This happy quality, as well as its sweet delicious flavor, has made the pecan one of the most popular and economically important nuts in America.

The pecan was discovered growing wild in America by the Indians, who not only ate the nutmeats, but used it to season hominy and corn cakes, to concoct a beverage, and to extract an oil for thickening venison broth. The word "pecan" comes, in fact, from the Indian word meaning "bone shell," and depending on the particular dialect of the Indian, the name was designated as pakan, pacaan, pecanne, pekaun, pagan, pagon, and pegan.

French ladies in New Orleans, who had nostalgic memories of their native praline— an almond covered with sugar—turned to pecans for cooking when they were unable to obtain almonds. Rich, crunchy, sweet pecan pralines gained an enthusiastic following and were among the delights the street vendors carried on trays through the Vieux Carré in the nineteenth century.

Sook's "Hankerings"

Sook carefully ordered her life around her "hankerings," her name for the activities that preoccupied her attention and time at certain months of the year. She posted a list of them on the kitchen wall and followed it faithfully.

FRUITCAKE

~~~~~~~~~~~~~~~~~~~~~~~~~~~~~~~~~~~

January and February: cut out pictures.

March: plant bulbs for the spring flowers.

April: make soft soap.

May: collect roots and herbs.

June: make dropsy medicine.

July: bake wedding cakes and give them away.

August and September: canning and preserving.

October: prepare fruitcakes.

November: fix cheese straws for Thanksgiving.

December: prepare Christmas decorations and gifts.

Pore Man's Fruitcake

This was the fruitcake that Sook gave to families that had a slew of children or were very poor.

1 cup butter

1-1/2 cups light brown sugar, firmly packed

4 eggs

3-1/2 cups sifted all-purpose flour

1/2 teaspoon baking soda

1 teaspoon salt

1 teaspoon ground cinnamon

1 teaspoon ground cloves

1 cup milk

16 ounces pitted dates, cut up

2 cups chopped pecans

1 cup candied cherries, halved

2 cups raisins

Beat butter and brown sugar together in a large bowl until blended. Add eggs, 1 at a time, beating well after each addition.

Sift flour, soda, salt, cinnamon and cloves together; add alternately with milk to butter sugar mixture. Beat until smooth and blended. Stir in dates, pecans, cherries and raisins.

Pour into greased and floured 10 x 4-inch tube pan. Bake at 300°F for 2 to 2-1/2 hours or until cake tests done. Let cake cool and remove from pan. Store several weeks in covered container before serving.

Rainbow Fruitcake

*Moist and light. Cuts easily into even,
fruit-studded slices.*

1-1/2 cups candied cherries

1 cup candied pineapple

1/2 cup chopped citron

1/2 cup chopped lemon peel

1/2 cup chopped range peel

1 cup light raisins

1 cup California walnuts

3 cups sifted all-purpose flour

1 cup butter

1 cup sugar

4 eggs

1/4 cup light corn syrup or pure maple syrup

1/4 cup orange juice

1/4 cup sherry (best)

Combine fruits and nuts; coat well with 1 cup of the flour.

Cream butter and sugar together until light and

fluffy. Add eggs, one at a time, beating well after each addition.

Combine corn syrup, orange juice and sherry; add alternately with remaining flour to creamed mixture. Fold in fruits and nut.

Pour batter into 6 well greased small loaf pans. Bake 70 to 80 minutes at 275° F. Let cake cool and place in an airtight container.

Rum Fruitcake

1 pound dried currants

1/2 pound dried citron,
    cut into thin slivers

1/2 pound dried figs,
    coarsely chopped

4 cups raisins

1-1/2 cups blanched almonds

1 cup cooked prunes,
    drained and chopped

1 cup pitted dates, chopped

1 cup candied cherries

1/2 cup diced candied orange peel

3 cups dark rum

1 cup butter

2 cups brown sugar, firmly packed

5 eggs

2 cups flour

2 teaspoons baking powder

1-1/2 teaspoons cinnamon

1-1/2 teaspoons nutmeg

1-1/2 allspice

1/2 teaspoon salt

Combine the first 9 ingredients in a large mixing
bowl (currants through orange peel). Pour rum

over the mixture and let it steep for at least 7 days, stirring occasionally.

Work butter until it is soft and gradually add the brown sugar, working the mixture until smooth. Beat in 2 eggs.

Sift flour with baking powder, cinnamon, nutmeg, allspice, and salt. Stir 1 cup of the flour mixture into the butter mixture. Beat in 3 eggs and add the rum-soaked fruits and nuts and the remaining flour mixture. Mix the batter thoroughly.

Spoon it in loaf pans (any size you choose) oiled, lined with brown paper, and oiled again. Bake the cakes in a very slow oven at 275°F for about 3 hours, or until the cakes test done.

Place the cakes on a wire rack until the cake are almost cool. Remove them from the pans and peel off the paper carefully. Wrap the cakes in cheesecloth and store them in an airtight container for about 1 month.

Fruitcake Flaming

1/2 cup brandy
6 large sugar cubes
2 teaspoons lemon juice

Fit a heat-proof cup or bowl in the center of the fruitcake and fill it with warmed brandy. Light the brandy and ladle the liquid over each serving of cake.

If you want to have a flame without using liquor, you may surround the fruitcake with cubes of sugar which have been soaked, but not drowned, in slightly warmed lemon extract. Use about 2 teaspoons lemon extract to 6 large cubes of sugar. Set a match to the sugar cubes.

Sem's Dark Fruitcake

1 cup orange juice

1/2 cup molasses

3 cups raisins

2 cups mixed, chopped,
    candied fruits and peels

1/2 cup butter

2/3 cup sugar

3 eggs

1-1/4 cups sifted flour

1/8 teaspoon soda

1 teaspoon cinnamon

1/2 teaspoon nutmeg

1/4 teaspoon allspice

1/4 teaspoon cloves

1/2 cup California walnuts

Combine orange juice with molasses and raisins
in a medium sauce pan. Cook over medium heat,
stirring occasionally until mixture comes to a boil.
Reduce heat and simmer 5 minutes. Remove

~~~~~~

from the heat; stir in the mixed fruits and peels.
Cream butter and sugar. Blend in eggs, one at a
time. Sift together flour, soda, cinnamon, nutmeg,
allspice, and cloves. Stir in creamed mixture, fruit
and peel mixture, and walnuts. Mix well till all
fruit is coated.

Line (1) 11 x 4 x 3-inch pan and (2) 5-1/2 x
3 x 2-1/4-inch pans with heavy paper, allowing
1/2 inch to extend above on all sides. Pour batter
into pans, filling about 3/4 full. Bake in very slow
oven at 275°F—about 2-1/2 hours for a large
loaf and about 1-1/2 hours for smaller loaves.

Cool cakes in pans, remove, and wrap in
brandy soaked cheesecloth. Pack in airtight containers. Every week or so sprinkle the cake with
brandy. Makes about 3-1/2 pounds of fruitcake.

*Dark fruitcake is a traditional Groom's cake, meant
to be cut into tiny pieces, boxed, be-ribboned, and*

given to each departing wedding guest. According to lore, every guest who took a piece home and tucked it under his pillow would have dreams of the future.

Sugar Frosted White Fruitcake

1/3 cup raisins

1/3 cup dark rum

1/3 cup sultanas

1/3 cup diced, mixed, glazed fruits

3 glazed red cherries, halved

3 glazed green cherries, halved

1-1/2 sticks (3/4 cup) butter, well softened

3/4 cup sugar

pinch of salt

3 eggs

1 teaspoon vanilla

1/4 teaspoon nutmeg

2 cups flour

1 tablespoon double-acting baking powder

2 tablespoons flour

1/4 cup chopped pecans

red glazed cherries

In a large bowl combine raisins, dark rum, sultanas, mixed glazed fruits, and cherries; allow to macerate for at least 6 hours, preferably overnight.

In another bowl combine butter, sugar, and salt; stir well. Beat in the eggs, 1 at a time and add the vanilla and nutmeg.

In another bowl sift together 2 cups of flour and the baking powder. Fold the flour mixture into the butter mixture, 1/4 at a time.

Drain the fruits in a sieve set over a bowl; add the rum to the batter. Dry the fruits on paper towels and toss them in a bowl with 2 tablespoons of flour. Shake the fruits in a sieve to rid them of excess flour and fold them into the batter, along with the pecans.

Pour the batter into a well buttered baking pan of 12 x 4-1/2 x 3-inches and bake the cake in a preheated hot oven at 375°F for 10 minutes. Reduce the heat to 325°F and bake the cake for 1-1/2 hours, or until it is well puffed and golden. Let the cake stand for 10 minutes, turn it out on a rack, and allow it to cool completely.

Place the rack over a shallow pan and spread sugar frosting over the cake. Decorate with red glazed cherries. Let frosting set for at least 1 hour.

Sugar Frosting

1 egg white
1 cup confectioners sugar
1 tablespoon lemon juice
pinch of salt

In a bowl beat the egg white until it is frothy. Sift in the confectioners sugar, add lemon juice and salt; beat the mixture for about 2 minutes, or until it is thick, but still of spreading consistency. Sift and beat in 1/4 cup more confectioners sugar if a thicker frosting is desired. Makes about 3/4 cup of frosting.

Toasted Almond Fruitcake

1/4 pound shelled almonds

2 tablespoons melted fat

1/2 cup butter

1/2 cup brown sugar

3 egg yolks, well beaten

1/4 cup molasses

3 egg whites

1 cup sifted cake flour

1/2 teaspoon salt

1 teaspoon allspice

1 teaspoon cinnamon

1/4 teaspoon nutmeg

1/4 teaspoon mace

1/8 teaspoon baking soda

2 cups seeded raisins

2 cups sultana raisins

3/4 cups currants

1 tablespoon preserved lemon
rind, cut small

1 tablespoon preserved orange
rind, cut small

1/4 pound glace cherries,
cut small

1/4 pound preserved pineapple,
cut small

3/8 pound thinly sliced citron

1/2 cup strawberry preserves

1/4 cup grape juice

Cover the almonds with boiling water and let stand five minutes; drain and slip off skins. Place almonds in a large shallow pan with the melted fat and bake to a golden brown in a moderately hot oven of 375°F for approximately 20 minutes; chop coarsely.

Meantime work the butter with a spoon until creamy and fluffy; add the brown sugar gradually. Combine with the beaten egg yolks and molasses; beat well with a spoon. Fold in the stiffly beaten egg whites.

Sift together flour, salt, spices, and baking soda, reserving 1/4 cup of mixture for dredging fruit. Add remaining flour mixture to the egg mixture. Combine the fruits which have been dredged with the 1/4 cup flour mixture, the strawberry preserves, toasted chopped almonds, and grape juice; stir until mixed.

Bake at 275°F in large loaf pan for about 4 hours. Store in tight tin container with 2 layers of

cheesecloth soaked in brandy or wine (your choice). Best when about three or four months old.

Magic of Christmas

There is magic in Christmas.

Candles are lighted and once again people join hands

to celebrate the birth of Christ. On Christmas day,

some make a ceremony of gift giving. Some do not,

they make it a day of prayer and blessing. This is the

universal season of joy and forgiveness, of high expectations and nostalgic delight. Christmas is not Christmas without a gala-board, without family and friends to share this happy occasion.

The table is the heart of holiday entertainment, whether it is set for a shimmering candlelight supper for two or a bountiful buffet for twenty. After your Christmas tree, your table is the most important decoration in the home, so give it a festive fancy-dress setting. Give it a theme and a color schemata, a touch of romance or fun or good cheer, all in keeping with the feast. Remember, you don't have to have saint figurines and poinsettias to set a Christmas table.

This is the time of year when even the most frostbitten pragmatist is set astir by the remembrance of Christmas past and the anticipation of Christmas to come.

As the routine drama of daily life is put aside in

favor of old-fashioned theatricality, a flurry of convivial plotting sweeps through the house as it is transformed into a fragrant evergreen bower with festoons of red-berried holly and gray-white mistletoe. Iridescent varicolored ornaments—delicate angels with gossamer wings and twinkling halos, merry little gnomes, and Saint Nicholas—glimmer in the tree and Christmas begins. Home is the setting for the Christmas drama—one of the leading performers is the dinner table.

White Fruitcake
with
Milk Icing

"Christmas without fruitcake would not be Christmas."
Fruitcakes, rich with fruits, nuts, and spirits, have come
to epitomize the festive season.

Truman Capote reported that in 1968 a fruitcake very much like this one was served by Cardel
Ltd. on crystal dessert plates to customers at their
615 Madison Avenue, New York City location.

1 cup butter	2 cups flour
1 cup sugar	1 teaspoon salt
5 eggs	1-1/2 teaspoon baking powder

FRUITCAKE

1/4 cup unsweetened pineapple juice

1/4 cup citron, finely cut

1/4 pound each orange peel and lemon peel, finely cut

1/2 cup chopped candied pineapple

1-1/4 cups chopped dates

1/2 chopped dried apricots

1/2 cup chopped figs

1/2 pound white raisins

2-1/4 pound cans moist shredded coconut

2 cups sliced, blanched almond meats

Thoroughly cream butter and sugar; add eggs, 1 at a time, beating well after each addition.

Reserve 1/2 cup flour for fruits; add remaining flour sifted with salt and baking powder alternately with pineapple juice. Add floured fruits, coconut and nut meats; stir until well blended.

Pour into 5 waxed paper-lined 3-1/2 x 7-1/2-inch loaf pans. Bake at 275°F for 1-1/2 hours.

Milk Icing

This is an old timey recipe and is probably not used much today, but it makes a beautiful topping for this cake when the snow white icing is decorated with whole red candied cherries.

1 teaspoon butter	1/2 cup whole milk
1-1/2 cups sugar	1/2 teaspoon vanilla

In a saucepan melt butter, then stir in sugar and milk. Cook, stirring constantly, until the mixture comes to a boil. Continue boiling, without stirring, until a drop tested in cold water forms a soft ball (the mixture will test at 234°F on a candy thermometer).

Allow the icing to cool, then beat until it reaches a spreading consistency. Add the vanilla, then frost the cake.

The Faulk Household

The house on Alabama Avenue in Monroeville, Alabama, was the home of Jenny Faulk and her sisters, Sook and Callie, and her brother, Bud. At the time of the death of my parents, it had housed three generations. My sisters,

Mary Ida, Lucille, and Lillie Mae, and our brother
Seaborn, went to live in the house with Jenny after
our parent's death. When Lillie Mae, who was the
oldest, married and had a son, Truman Persons,
she brought him to be raised by the Faulk family
on Alabama Avenue.

The most important people in the Faulk household were mainly the housekeepers, cooks, and
mammies. Sam Muscadine was a cook of extraor-
dinary talents and always came to the house for
special occasions. He lived in a room of a long-
deserted plantation house on Little River. To him
it was home. The only home he had ever known.
When he was summoned by the Faulks, he always
wore his "misbehavin'" coat, a frock tailcoat he had
been given by a plantation owner, long ago. When
he walked it stood straight out in the wind. Sam
was not a big man. He walked with a walk of pride:
strutting along with his gold headed walking

cane—another gift. His face was so wrinkled it made you think of crumpled cobwebs. His nose was flat and wide as a pancake: his eyes were like saucers. He was "Jesus Fever" in Truman's novel *Other Voices, Other Rooms*. We loved his comings and goings. When he came he always brought a gift of wild honey in a tin pail. This honey came from the swamp and had a musty taste that was dark and almost forbidding. Never have I ever tasted anything that would come near to his honey!

The most important servants in the household were Anna Stabler and Corrie Wolff. Anna and Corrie used an outhouse with a small square window and it stood directly behind a thirty-foot black walnut tree. So, the view was blocked and it was impossible to see if the outhouse was occupied. It was the ideal place to hide and play with the "nutting stones." These were stone slabs with marked

indentations for holding nuts to be cracked. We were cunning children and when someone was in the outhouse we would gather up long sticks and poke them up through the holes. A slight tickle, and the occupant would cry out because it felt like a snake or a big red-bellied spider.

We were always careful that it was not Anna Stabler because we knew the penalty for poking a stick at her. Only once did we make that mistake. Anna came out of nowhere, ripped a switch off the peach tree, and wrapped it around our legs. I have never seen such perfect aim as it curled around our bare legs leaving livid red marks. Then Anna said calmly, "Them red marks 'round yore legs will remind you every day of what hell is like."

Anna was a huge hulk of a woman . . . and mean! She was in charge of the servants, children, and entire household, including Jenny. A deep scar ran across her left cheek from the tip of her ear to

her chin—the result of a fight at the church supper over a man. At the drop of a hat she would tell everybody "Dere's no sweeter place to lay for love 'dan in a fresh haymow. Gawd, jist smellin' dat mixture of horse an' hay is purely like bitin' into unexpected pepper."

Corrie Wolf was a quadroon—second in command. She lived in a little house behind the big house in the old slave quarters known as "Tote Road." It was so called because in the time of slaves they traveled back and forth to the house by this little road as they carried goodies from the kitchen back to their quarters. Corrie was a constant source of enjoyment for children. She practiced voodoo and claimed to be a direct descendant of Dr. Yah Yah, a voodoo doctor in New Orleans back around 1850. She was always making crosses out of red root and hanging them on the front door of the house (until Jenny found them) to block the pas-

sage of evil spirits into the house. Her "bottle trees" were a work of art. She saved all the blue bottles, green bottles, and any other color she could luck upon, to select a tree with strong limbs. She would take the bottles and put them well over the limb. This would catch evil spirits and they would not be able to get out. When the sun struck her trees, they were something to see and strangers always asked, "what in the world?"

With all of her queer ways, we still loved to go to the kitchen when Corrie was there because she would always let us roll out cookies, or make a "try" cake from a bit of leftover batter. The most fun was making "thimble biscuits." Children brought up in the South during the first half of the twentieth century were weaned on tales of "plat eyes, haints, spirits and ghosts." Black people lived in a universe made all the more frightening by the presence of a host of devils, witches, and bad luck

spirits. Corrie was full of black folk wisdom. "Don't y'all spit in de fire," Corrie would warn us children. "It will dry up yore lungs." "Don't go out of de house on a dark night, cause de branches of a tree will reach down an' carry yo' away."

Corrie was in great demand at "birthings" because she owned a string of beads, which looked like unpolished rubies, emeralds and amethysts, and aided a woman when she was about to give birth. Corrie claimed they had come all the way from Africa and had been passed down to her by way of her illustrious predecessor Dr. Yah Yah. Many nights Corrie would be called upon to get her birthing beads and go down to Rooktown to deliver a baby. When Corrie opened the door it mattered not that it was a white man or a black man, the plea was always the same, "Come on Corrie, git yore birthin' beads an' come wid me, fo' gawd's sake.

The first thing Corrie did upon arriving was to place the beads around the woman's neck, making sure they touched her naked skin, and then she pulled them down tightly between the woman's breasts. Corrie then drew the quilt snugly up under the woman's neck and allowed no one to enter the room. Later, after the beads had worked their magic, Corrie would help in the actual birth. She always had some fresh spider webs handy, "cause a life can leak out fast an' de spider web can dam it up an' hol' it fast."

Corrie could predict a child's nature depending on the phases of the tide and moon at the time of birth. A child born at the time of a new moon would be contrary and troublesome all its life. Any child born on the rising tide would more than likely be a male.

Next Corrie would have a man get her a good sharp ax. The blade had to be clean and without

rust. This she placed under the woman's bed to cut the labor pains—rust on the blade, however, would make the labor long and drawn out.

After the birth, the celebration began. It was like a big carnival. There was singing and dancing. Open fires roared under big black iron kettles. "I'se got a whole hawg an' a bishelo' rice a-cookin'" a black man with a pockmarked face would holler out as he stirred his great iron kettle.

As soon as Corrie announced the sex of the child the dancing started. Every skirt was spinning and twirling. When the dance called out "sashay all!" it was time for Corrie to leave because it was then the party would get wilder and wilder and go on into the wee morning hours.

Coming from such a rich place in the world, how was it possible for Truman Capote to be other than the wonderful writer that he was? Truman wrote in "One Christmas," "Back home [Alabama] I was

used to fried chicken and collard greens and butter beans and corn bread and other comforting things." How is it possible to describe Southern food better?